KEN GRIFFEY JR.
CENTER FIELDER

SEATTLE
MARINERS

ALEX RODRIGUEZ
SHORTSTOP

SEATTLE
MARINERS

# THE STORY OF THE SEATTLE MARINERS

Published by Creative Education
P.O. Box 227, Mankato, Minnesota 56002
Creative Education is an imprint of The Creative Company
www.thecreativecompany.us

Design and production by Blue Design
Art direction by Rita Marshall
Printed by Corporate Graphics in the United States of America

Photographs by Getty Images (Kimberly Barth/AFP, B. Bennett, Bernstein Associates, Jonathan Daniel, Terry Donnelly, Stephen Dunn, Charles Franklin/MLB Photos, Otto Greule Jr, Otto Greule Jr./Allsport, Harry How, Robert Leiter/MLB Photos, Dan Levine/AFP, Daniel Lippitt/AFP, Lonnie Major/Allsport, Jim McIsaac, National Baseball Hall of Fame Library/MLB Photos, Doug Pensinger, Rich Pilling/MLB Photos, John Reid III/MLB Photos, Rick Stewart, Rick Stewart/Allsport, John Williamson/MLB Photos)

Library of Congress Cataloging-in-Publication Data

LeBoutillier, Nate.
The story of the Seattle Mariners / by Nate LeBoutillier.
p. cm. — (Baseball: the great American game)
Includes index.
Summary: The history of the Seattle Mariners professional baseball team from its inaugural 1977 season to today, spotlighting the team's greatest players and most memorable moments.
ISBN 978-1-60818-056-1
1. Seattle Mariners (Baseball team)—History—Juvenile literature. I. Title. II. Series.

GV875.S42L43 2011
796.357'6409797772—dc22          2010025476

CPSIA: 110310 PO1381

First Edition
9 8 7 6 5 4 3 2 1

*Page 3: Third baseman Adrian Beltre*
*Page 4: Right fielder Ichiro Suzuki*

BASEBALL: THE GREAT AMERICAN GAME

# THE STORY
# OF THE
# SEATTLE
# MARINERS

*Nate LeBoutillier*

CREATIVE EDUCATION

# CONTENTS

# PILOTING A TEAM

On November 13, 1851, the schooner *Exact*, carrying a group of explorers led by civil engineer and surveyor Arthur Denny, landed at Alki Point on the west coast of North America. *Alki*, a Chinook Indian word meaning "by and by," seemed to be an apt description of the point of land, which had been around, of course, for centuries, but was one of the last areas to be built into a large city—what became Seattle, Washington—by white pioneers in the settlement of America's West.

Today, the Seattle area hosts a thriving population of more than 3 million people and is known as both a hotbed of rock music and as the birthplace of the United States' foremost aeronautics company, Boeing. Seattle has earned many nicknames, including the "Queen City of the Pacific" (reflecting early settlers' hopefulness), the "Emerald City" (because of the lushness of the area's trees), and "Rain City" (due to the frequent rainfall experienced in the region). Since 1977, Seattle has also earned a reputation as a baseball town. That year, a new American League (AL) team called the Mariners put down roots in the Pacific Northwest.

Downtown Seattle's signature building is the distinctive, 605-foot-tall Space Needle, which was built as part of the 1962 World's Fair.

## PITCHER · RANDY JOHNSON

With his penetrating scowl, enormous wingspan, and tendency to unleash a wild pitch now and then, Johnson was arguably the most intimidating man ever to set foot on a pitcher's mound. At 6-foot-10, he was also (at the time) the tallest pitcher ever to play in the major leagues. Johnson's nearly 100-mile-per-hour heater, combined with a brutal slider, made "The Big Unit" a devastating power pitcher for the better part of two decades. In 1995, one of the best years of his Mariners career, the rangy southpaw hurled a complete-game three-hitter that clinched Seattle's first division title and playoff berth.

**RANDY JOHNSON**
PITCHER

SEATTLE MARINERS

### STATS

Mariners seasons: 1989–98

Height: 6-foot-10

Weight: 225

- 10-time All-Star

- 5-time Cy Young Award winner

- 303–166 career record

- 4,875 career strikeouts

The Mariners were not Seattle's first foray into major league baseball. The city hosted a major-league club in 1969 named the Pilots. Financial constraints, stadium issues, and a dismal 64–98 record doomed the franchise, though, and it moved to Milwaukee, Wisconsin, before the following season and was renamed the Brewers. Seven years later, Major League Baseball gave the Washington metropolis another chance with a new franchise. "Mariners" was a fitting choice of name, given the region's history of maritime commerce, and the new club unveiled uniforms of royal blue, gold, and baby blue. For its first manager, the team hired former big-league catcher Darrell Johnson.

The first official player in Mariners history was center fielder Ruppert Jones, who was chosen in a special expansion draft in 1976. Alongside the fleet-footed Jones, the "M's" planted veteran right fielder Leroy Stanton. The infield was populated by talented youngsters such as shortstop Craig Reynolds, second baseman Julio Cruz, and first baseman Dan Meyer, and the pitching staff—which would prove to be Seattle's weakest link— featured such hurlers as Dick Pole, Diego Segui, and Gary Wheelock.

The new club played its first game on April 6, 1977, in front of a sold-out crowd at the Kingdome, Seattle's indoor home stadium. On the mound was Segui, a Cuban right-hander who had played for the Seattle Pilots. The game ended in a 7–0 whitewash at the hands of the California Angels—one of many Seattle defeats that season. Even though the duo of Jones and Stanton combined to slug 51 homers, the team finished the year 64–98, second-to-last in the AL Western Division.

In 1978, first baseman Bruce Bochte joined the Mariners and became an instant star, batting well above .300. And the Mariners were lucky for it. "In the beginning, I was the only one hitting the ball," Bochte later recalled. "It got to the point that I felt if I didn't get two hits and drive in two runs, we wouldn't win the game." The pressure seemed to send Bochte into a slump, and the Mariners ended the season in last place.

Things improved in 1979 when slick-hitting left fielder Willie Horton came aboard and clubbed 29 home runs. Seattle hosted baseball's annual All-Star Game that year, and Bochte delighted the home crowd by driving in a run in the "Midseason Classic." The first baseman also posted 106 runs batted in (RBI) during the season, helping the Mariners earn 11 more wins than they had the year before.

# LEROY STANTON

Leroy Stanton joined Seattle toward the end of his big-league career, having spent his best years with the California Angels. Although never a superstar, he was capable of highlight-reel home runs and terrific outfield throws.

# ONE-YEAR WONDERS

Seattle's first big-league baseball team was the Pilots, named to commemorate the area's maritime and aviation history. The Pilots joined the AL in 1969, but by the next season, they had been moved and reborn as the Milwaukee Brewers. The club was an oddity as the only major-league team in decades to relocate after just a single season. It had happened only once before in the 20th century—ironically, to the original Milwaukee Brewers, who became the St. Louis Browns after the 1901 season. The Pilots were also the first major-league team to declare bankruptcy, mostly due to

low fan attendance at games. The club's home opener was attended by Washington governor Dan Evans, AL president Joe Cronin, and even famous cowboy actor Gene Autry. Basking in the limelight, the Pilots beat the Chicago White Sox 7–0. But ticket prices were among the highest in baseball, the home field Sick's Stadium was in bad condition, and injuries plagued the team as it lost 22 of 28 games in August. Interest in the Pilots has grown in recent years, due in part to the 1970 book *Ball Four* by pitcher Jim Bouton, which offers an insider's look at the team and has become something of a classic.

## CATCHER · DAN WILSON

As a young Cincinnati Reds fan growing up in Chicago, Wilson spent time in elementary school drawing catchers in his notebooks and worshiping Reds backstop Johnny Bench. His dream of making it to the big leagues came true when he joined the Mariners in 1994. After a slow 1995 season, Wilson's natural talents emerged when the feisty catcher earned more playing time, slammed 18 home runs, and made the 1996 All-Star team. But defense was really Wilson's specialty, as he threw out 39 percent of would-be base stealers and led the AL in putouts at catcher in 1996.

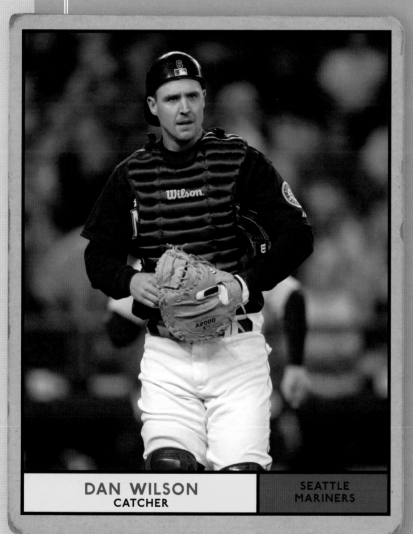

DAN WILSON
CATCHER

SEATTLE
MARINERS

### STATS

Mariners seasons: 1994–2005

Height: 6-foot-3

Weight: 200

• 88 career HR

• 519 career RBI

• 1996 All-Star

• .995 career fielding percentage

## FIRST BASEMAN · ALVIN DAVIS

"Mr. Mariner," Alvin Davis, was named the AL Rookie of the Year when he slugged 27 home runs and posted 116 RBI in 1984. The only Mariners player to win a major award in the club's first dozen years, Davis set or tied team records for most RBI, walks, and home runs by a rookie. Hitting most of his homers in the friendly confines of Seattle's Kingdome, the smooth-swinging left-hander was a huge fan favorite in the franchise's early years. His sharp batting eye led to many walks, often raising his on-base percentage more than 100 points above his batting average.

ALVIN DAVIS
FIRST BASEMAN

SEATTLE
MARINERS

### STATS

Mariners seasons: 1984–91

Height: 6-foot-1

Weight: 195

- .280 career BA

- 3-time Mariners team MVP

- 1984 AL Rookie of the Year

- 1984 All-Star

# THE STARS COME OUT

he 1980 and 1981 seasons were disappointments in Seattle, as even the fine efforts of lefty hurler Floyd Bannister, outfielders Jeff Burroughs and Dave Henderson, and the ever-productive Bochte could not keep the club from backsliding. California real estate tycoon George Argyros purchased the team in 1981 and quickly reduced salaries, making his players among the lowest-paid in the majors. As the Mariners ended the strike-shortened 1981 season with only 44 wins, cheers were few in Seattle.

In 1982, under new manager Rene Lachemann, the Mariners began to shore up their pitching staff, which helped boost the club's record to 76–86. Perhaps the most prominent name in the rotation was Gaylord Perry, who had already spent 20 seasons in the big leagues and acquired the nickname "The Ancient Mariner" in Seattle. That season, the 43-year-old hurler celebrated his 300th career win. Perry, who would eventually enter the Baseball Hall of Fame, was a notorious spitballer (a pitcher who illegally spits on the ball before throwing it in order to affect pitches' movement) and was once quoted as saying, "I reckon I tried everything on

the old apple but salt and pepper and chocolate sauce topping."

The Mariners spent the mid-1980s trying to add young talent. In 1984, first baseman Alvin Davis finished the season with 27 home runs and 116 RBI. Crafty southpaw pitcher Mark Langston, meanwhile, became the first rookie in 30 years to lead the AL in strikeouts, fanning 204 batters. Injuries plagued the Mariners in 1985 and 1986 as the team posted its 9th and 10th straight losing records. Fan attendance at the Kingdome waned as the losses mounted.

A new sense of optimism took hold in Seattle in 1987 as the Mariners produced a club-record 78 wins behind the All-Star trio of Langston, second baseman Harold Reynolds, and third baseman Jim Presley. Langston won 19 games with a 3.84 earned run average (ERA), while the speedy Reynolds stole a club-record 60 bases. Reynolds won the Gold Glove award the next year despite leading all AL second basemen in errors, since he also led the league in assists and double plays. The award made headlines as perennial honoree Frank White of the

# HAROLD REYNOLDS

Harold Reynolds was a native of the Pacific Northwest, born and raised in neighboring Oregon. Although he was a more than capable hitter, he truly earned his paychecks with reliable defense and aggressive base running.

## SECOND BASEMAN · HAROLD REYNOLDS

A defensive stalwart with excellent speed and fielding range, Reynolds led all AL second basemen in games started, fielding chances, putouts, assists, and double plays in 1987. The powerful switch hitter was also terrific at the plate, a keen-eyed batter who rarely struck out and steadily improved his batting average as his career went along. The ever-smiling, community-conscious Reynolds won the 1991 Roberto Clemente Award for his outstanding work with young baseball players. Reynolds retired in 1994, trading in his baseball jersey for a sports jacket to become a television baseball analyst.

**HAROLD REYNOLDS**
SECOND BASEMAN

SEATTLE
MARINERS

### STATS

**Mariners seasons: 1983–92**

**Height: 5-foot-11**

**Weight: 165**

• **2-time All-Star**

• **3-time Gold Glove winner**

• **1987 AL leader in stolen bases (60)**

• **1988 AL leader in triples (11)**

Kansas City Royals was livid at the selection, putting Reynolds in an uncomfortable position. "I was totally shocked to win the Gold Glove," Reynolds admitted. "But what was I supposed to do? Give it back?"

The Mariners seemed ready to set sail after rookie third baseman Edgar Martinez joined the squad in 1987. Martinez combined slugging power with a keen batting eye, and he would hit over .300 in his first three full seasons in Seattle. As Minnesota Twins star Kirby Puckett once helpfully told a reporter who was writing about the third-sacker, "You can save a lot of room in your column by just saying three words: hit, hit, hit."

Still, Argyros was becoming impatient. "We are no longer an expansion team," the owner said. "It's time we started winning." In 1988, strapping outfielder Jay Buhner, nicknamed "Bone" because of his shaved head, came to Seattle from the New York Yankees and did his part to jump-start a new era of winning. But even he knew the Mariners had their work cut out for them when he saw the sparse attendance at home games. "The Kingdome was so empty," he later recalled, "you could hear the crickets chirping from the upper decks."

KEN JR.

## LIKE FATHER, LIKE SON

On August 31, 1990, the Seattle Mariners made family history. For the first time, a father and son—outfielders Ken Griffey Sr. and Ken Griffey Jr.—played in the same major-league lineup. The 40-year-old and 20-year-old, batting second and third in Seattle's lineup, did not disappoint. In the first inning, the packed Kingdome crowd rose to its feet when Griffey Sr. knocked a hit up the middle for a single, and it jumped up again when Griffey Jr. ripped a single to right field. When Griffey Sr. scored the first run of the game on a hit by first baseman Alvin Davis, and Griffey Jr. scored the second run just a few minutes later, the place went wild. In the sixth inning, the elder Griffey showed his son how it was done in the field, throwing out Kansas City Royals outfielder Bo Jackson, who was trying to stretch a single into a double. Griffey Jr. hunched down on his hands and knees in center field and broke into a beaming smile as Jackson was tagged. "I wanted to cry," Junior said. "It was my dad's day." The father-son duo led the Mariners to a 5–2 win that day and played together in a total of 51 games.

MARINERS

# JUNIOR TO THE RESCUE

I n 1989, the Mariners traded Langston and replaced him with towering young pitcher Randy Johnson. Also new to the roster that season was an effervescent, 19-year-old center fielder named Ken Griffey Jr., known to fans simply as "Junior." Griffey had it all: brilliant defensive skills, effortless speed, and prodigious hitting power. In the 11 seasons that followed, Griffey would become one of baseball's most popular stars and spark Seattle to increasing success. "I don't think anybody has ever been that good at that age," said Mariners batting coach Gene Clines.

In a dominant performance, the 6-foot-10 Johnson recorded the franchise's first no-hitter on June 2, 1990. That was the start of great things, as Johnson would go on to post a 130–74 record for Seattle over the next 10 years. Along with Buhner, Seattle's "Big Three" of Johnson, Martinez, and Griffey propelled the 1990 Mariners to a respectable 77–85 mark.

Seattle's fortunes continued to rise in 1991 as the Mariners managed a winning record for the first time in their history, finishing the season 83–79. "We're not losers anymore!" yelled Alvin Davis as the Kingdome crowd went wild after victory number 81. So enthusiastic was the fans' response that Dave Niehaus, who had been the Mariners' radio broadcaster since 1977, noted, "It was like we'd won the World Series."

Expectations rose higher as former big-league outfielder Lou Piniella was then hired as Seattle's manager. The fiery Piniella had skippered the Cincinnati Reds to a 1990 World Series title, and Seattle fans hoped he would bring the same magic to the Mariners. It would not happen right away, though, as a winning 1993 season (82–80) was sandwiched between two losing ones.

During a game in July 1994, four large ceiling tiles crashed down from the Kingdome roof, forcing the Mariners onto the longest road trip in franchise history—20 away games in 21 days. As the team embarked on the grueling schedule, Seattle officials began discussing a proposal to build a new baseball stadium. Rumors also began to swirl that the Mariners might relocate to the greener pastures of another city.

When Griffey was sidelined with a broken wrist, Seattle's 1995 season seemed in trouble. To get a much-needed boost on the mound, the Mariners then traded two minor-league prospects to the San Diego Padres for

## THIRD BASEMAN · EDGAR MARTINEZ

When the Seattle Mariners were in danger of being relocated in 1995, Edgar Martinez came to the rescue. His series-clinching double down the left-field line in the AL Division Series (ALDS) helped propel the Mariners to a new level of popularity in Seattle. A skilled fielder and patient hitter, Martinez—known as "Papi" or "Gar" to his teammates—usually looked over several pitches before deciding which one to attack. The soft-spoken native of Puerto Rico earned renown as one of the AL's top designated hitters but also spent nearly 600 games manning third base. Martinez was inducted into the Mariners team Hall of Fame in 2007.

**EDGAR MARTINEZ**
THIRD BASEMAN

SEATTLE
MARINERS

### STATS

| | |
|---|---|
| **Mariners seasons: 1987–2004** | |
| **Height: 6 feet** | |
| **Weight: 218** | |

- **7-time All-Star**
- **6 seasons of 100-plus RBI**
- **2-time AL leader in BA**
- **309 career HR**

## THE DOUBLE

One of the most memorable moments in Mariners history happened in the deciding Game 5 of the 1995 ALDS. It was the bottom of the 11th inning, and Seattle trailed the New York Yankees 5–4. Mariners second baseman Joey Cora was on third base, center fielder Ken Griffey Jr. was on first, and powerful designated hitter Edgar Martinez was at the plate. Yankees pitcher Jack McDowell delivered, and Martinez smoked a line drive down the Kingdome's left-field line. Griffey, flying at the crack of the bat, touched second base before the ball even hit the outfield wall. The Seattle crowd stood as one as Cora sped for home with Griffey suddenly hot on his heels. Cora touched home, Griffey slid across the plate in a dusty blur, and the Mariners won the game 6–5, setting off a joyful explosion in the Kingdome. Martinez's clutch two-bagger has since been immortalized as simply "The Double." That one hit sent Seattle to its first AL Championship Series (ALCS) and helped revive enthusiasm for a new Mariners stadium. Dave Niehaus, the Mariners' play-by-play radio announcer, summed up the famous moment by saying, "That was the biggest hit in Mariners history."

reliable pitcher Andy Benes. "We really feel that this is the big year for us with the pennant race and the Wild Card race," said Mariners executive Roger Jongewaard.

By August, the Mariners were 13 games behind the California Angels in the AL West standings. But an Angels losing streak then coincided with a Mariners winning rampage. Behind veterans such as Johnson, Martinez, and catcher Dan Wilson, Seattle miraculously charged back, defeating the Angels 9–1 in a special one-game playoff to secure its first division title. The underdog Mariners then kept right on rolling in the playoffs, beating the Yankees in an ALDS marked by one of the most exciting finishes in postseason history. In the deciding Game 5, Griffey—back from his injury—slammed a home run in the eighth inning to send the game into extra innings, then slid home with the game-winning run on a Martinez double in the bottom of the 11th.

Baseball hysteria in Seattle reached a fever pitch as the team was victorious in two of the first three ALCS games against the Cleveland

Indians. The excitement subsided, though, as the Indians swept the next three games to capture the pennant. The year was over in Seattle, but what a ride it had been. That 1995 campaign is still fondly remembered in Seattle as "The Magical Season."

In 1996, the Mariners added to their lineup an extraordinary rookie shortstop named Alex Rodriguez. "A-Rod," as he was known, was both large and graceful, with a powerful arm and an explosive bat. "Alex has a good chance to be the best shortstop ever," said Baltimore Orioles Hall of Fame shortstop Cal Ripken Jr. Seattle's star-studded lineup went on to win a team-record 85 games that season, but a second-place finish in the division left the Mariners out of the postseason.

Randy Johnson was among baseball's top stories in 1997, as he notched a 20–4 record with 291 strikeouts. Seattle's mighty offense also clobbered a franchise-record 264 home runs that year, and the team sent 5 players to the All-Star Game: Johnson, Griffey, Martinez, Rodriguez, and 5-foot-8 second baseman Joey Cora. The Mariners' season ended with another AL West championship and a return to the postseason, but the team quickly fell to the Orioles in the first

ALEX RODRIGUEZ

## SHORTSTOP · ALEX RODRIGUEZ

"A-Rod" was one of baseball's brightest stars almost immediately upon joining the Mariners at 18 years of age, quickly proving himself a superb all-around player who could hit, field, run, and throw equally well. Tall, long-armed, and powerful, Rodriguez could hit almost any pitch for a home run. In 1998, he became just the third member (after All-Stars Jose Canseco and Barry Bonds) of the "40-40" club (40 home runs and 40 stolen bases in 1 season), racking up 42 dingers and 46 steals. He won four Silver Slugger awards as baseball's top-hitting shortstop during his seven years with the Mariners.

### STATS

Mariners seasons: 1994–2000

Height: 6-foot-3

Weight: 225

- 3-time AL MVP

- 2-time Gold Glove winner

- 301 career stolen bases

- 5-time AL leader in HR

**ALEX RODRIGUEZ**
SHORTSTOP

SEATTLE
MARINERS

round of the playoffs. The playoff loss stung, but there was good news, too: Griffey was named the AL Most Valuable Player (MVP), and construction began on a new stadium that would ensure the Mariners remained in Seattle.

# CHANGE OF COURSE

In 1998, Mariners pitcher Jamie Moyer earned his 100th career win and 1,000th strikeout, and Griffey became the youngest player ever to slam his 350th home run. Still, the season ended in disappointment, as the club finished 11 and a half games out of first place in the AL West.

The main highlight of the 1999 season occurred on July 15, when the Mariners moved into Safeco Field, their new, state-of-the-art stadium in downtown Seattle. The gorgeous park, built at a cost of $517 million, was created to draw more fans and enable Seattle to sign more top-notch players. Many Seattle fans were therefore left puzzled—and heartbroken— when the club parted with two of its greatest heroes. By 1999, fans had bid

## LEFT FIELDER · JAY BUHNER

Jay Buhner had his flaws. He led the AL in strikeouts in 1996 and 1997, and he was so slow afoot that he managed just six stolen bases in his career. But the outfielder made up for those shortcomings with his home run power, clubhouse leadership, and cannon of a throwing arm. Seattle fans adored Buhner—recognizable by his shaved head and wraparound sunglasses—for his friendly personality and great passion for the game. He primarily manned right field but spent time in left as well and played defense with such intensity that even his slow feet could not keep him from winning a Gold Glove award in 1996.

### STATS

Mariners seasons: 1988–2001

Height: 6-foot-3

Weight: 205

- 965 career RBI

- 3 seasons of 40-plus HR

- 1996 All-Star

- .383 BA in 1995 playoffs

**JAY BUHNER**
LEFT FIELDER

SEATTLE
MARINERS

# CRASHING THE PARTY

Beginning in the 1960s and reaching new heights of popularity in the late '70s, numerous major league baseball teams employed cartoonish, costumed mascots to inspire and entertain ticket buyers. Seattle created its own mascot, named Mariner Moose, for this purpose in 1990, but while the Moose has elicited countless smiles, he has also occasionally caused winces and shudders. In 1995, while wearing in-line skates and being towed with a ski rope behind an ATV across the Kingdome outfield, Mariner Moose was sent hurtling at high speed toward the center-field wall when the tow rope snapped.

The ensuing crash left the Moose with a broken leg, and he had to be carried off the field. In 1997, Mariner Moose and the ATV again combined to provide a scary moment when the Moose—this time riding the ATV—inadvertently clipped Boston Red Sox outfielder Coco Crisp, who only avoided serious injury by athletically jumping mostly out of the way. The Red Sox were not amused, but Crisp forgave the accident-prone mascot. "I'm not an angry person," said Crisp. "I'm not going to run over and go clothesline the guy. It was an accident. I'm sure he didn't mean to try and take me out."

RANDY JOHNSON

farewell to both Randy Johnson and Ken Griffey Jr., who left to sign bigger contracts with other teams.

As the 21st century began, new center fielder Mike Cameron wowed fans with his incredible glove work and solid hitting. Other talented newcomers included pitcher Freddy Garcia, third baseman David Bell, and Kazuhiro Sasaki, a closer from Japan who anchored the bullpen with 37 saves in 2000. This crew surprised fans by going 91–71, earning a Wild Card berth into the 2000 playoffs, sweeping the Chicago White Sox in the ALDS, and then pushing the Yankees to six games in the ALCS before finally falling.

Seattle fans were then left disappointed by the departure of yet another superstar when Rodriguez jumped to the Texas Rangers for the richest sports contract ever: $252 million for 10 seasons. "I see little connection between superstars and winning," Mariners official Howard Lincoln said, explaining the club's philosophy of balanced team play. "It turns players on to have a team where everyone is expected to contribute."

Two talented players, slugging second baseman Bret Boone and swift Japanese outfielder Ichiro Suzuki, joined the Mariners' roster in 2001. Boone finished the

Randy Johnson averaged more than 13 wins a year throughout his Mariners career and reigned as the AL's strikeout king for 4 straight seasons.

# BRET BOONE

season with a league-leading 141 RBI, an AL record for second basemen. Ichiro, meanwhile, put on a stunning all-around performance. The lithe, quiet right fielder with the laser throwing arm made a spectacular debut with a 23-game hitting streak in his first big-league season. Ichiro went on to win the AL Rookie of the Year award as well as the Gold Glove award for his excellent defense, becoming the first major-leaguer in 26 years to win such honors in the same season.

With the contributions of these new players, the 2001 Mariners dominated the AL West and set a new league record for wins in a season with 116, losing only 46 games all year. In the ALDS, the Mariners overcame a slow start to beat the Indians and advance to the ALCS versus the Yankees. Frustratingly, for the second year in a row, New York stopped Seattle, ending its storybook season by winning four of five games. Seattle fans didn't know it yet, but that was the last playoff action the Mariners would see for a while.

## CENTER FIELDER · KEN GRIFFEY JR.

Ken Griffey Jr., nicknamed "The Kid," was the darling of Mariners fans in the 1990s when the team emerged as a playoff contender and was voted "Player of the Decade" by his major-league peers. Griffey often made breathtaking, over-the-shoulder catches of the sort immortalized by New York Giants center fielder Willie Mays during the 1954 World Series. At the plate, he displayed one of the most effortlessly powerful swings of all time. "Junior" made history by playing on the same Mariners team as his talented outfielder father, Ken Griffey Sr., in 1990 and 1991. Father and son even hit back-to-back home runs on September 14, 1990.

**KEN GRIFFEY JR.**
CENTER FIELDER

SEATTLE
MARINERS

### STATS

**Mariners seasons: 1989–99, 2009–10**

**Height: 6-foot-3**

**Weight: 220**

- **13-time All-Star**

- **10-time Gold Glove winner**

- **1,836 career RBI**

- **630 career HR**

Longtime manager Lou Piniella jumped ship in 2002 to become skipper of his hometown Tampa Bay Devil Rays, and the Mariners hired Bob Melvin as his replacement. In 2003, Seattle led the division in the second half of the season but then saw the title slip away. For the second year in a row, the Mariners went an impressive 93–69 but missed the playoffs. Still, fans remained justly proud of their team and its fourth straight winning campaign. As one Mariners fan put it at season's end, "Showing up this weekend at Safeco is our way of saying, 'Hey, thanks for all the good times.'"

Although the Mariners fell to a disappointing 63–99 in 2004, there was at least one reason to celebrate. In October, Ichiro broke St. Louis Browns great George Sisler's single-season record of 257 hits, finishing with 262. "I'm not a big guy, or muscular," the Japanese-speaking outfielder said through a translator, "and hopefully kids will look at me and see that somebody with a regular body can get into the record books."

ICHIRO SUZUKI

# BOB MELVIN

Bob Melvin was a well-traveled backup catcher before going into managing, having suited up for seven different big-league teams. He managed the Mariners for two seasons, then became skipper of the Arizona Diamondbacks.

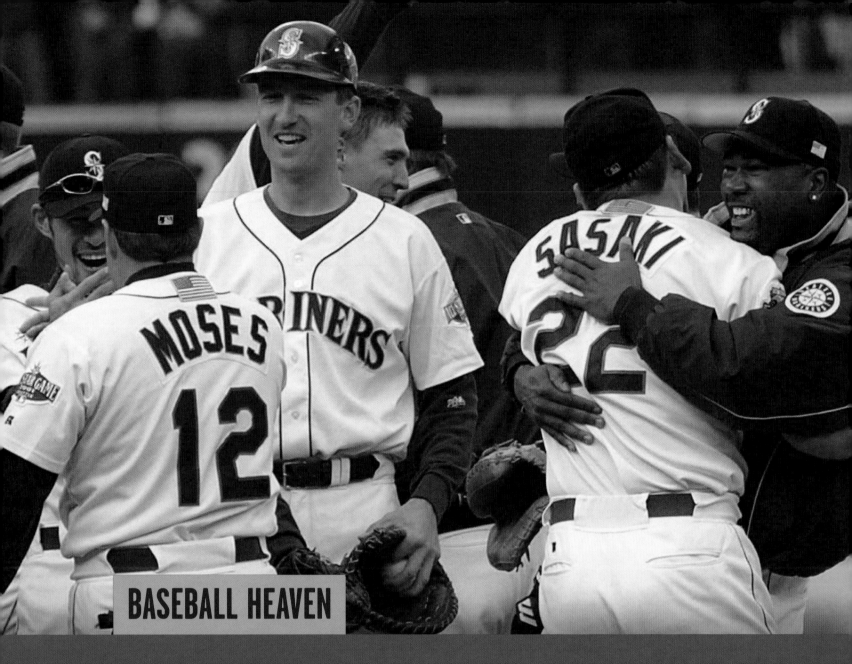

## BASEBALL HEAVEN

Before the 2001 season, no one could have guessed that the Seattle Mariners were about to become the first team since the 1906 Chicago Cubs to win 116 regular-season games and, in the process, captivate an entire city. Local enthusiasm became so great during the season that one Spokane Valley farmer even transformed a 14-acre cornfield into a maze shaped like the Mariners' compass logo. That "season in baseball heaven," as it is remembered in Mariners country, featured many stars. Ichiro Suzuki sustained an amazing 23-game hitting streak, Freddy Garcia notched 163 strikeouts, and Mike

Cameron hit 25 home runs. By early June, with Seattle leading the AL West by 19 games, the question was not whether Seattle would win the division but by how many games. Seattle fans were shocked when the Mariners fell behind the Cleveland Indians two games to one in the opening round of the playoffs. But manager Lou Piniella's crew came back to beat "the Tribe" in five games and reach the ALCS opposite the New York Yankees. The "Bronx Bombers" showed no respect for the record-setting Mariners, though, beating them in five games and putting an end to the dream season.

### RIGHT FIELDER · ICHIRO SUZUKI

After playing nine years with the Orix Blue Wave in Japan's Pacific League, Ichiro Suzuki became the first Japanese position player to sign with a major-league club. He topped the All-Star balloting in his rookie season (largely because fan voting was allowed in Japan) and earned the 2001 Rookie of the Year award. In the field, the slender Ichiro fired throws with laser precision, and he featured a most unique style at the plate. The momentum from his left-handed swing propelled him toward first base even as he was making contact, forcing infielders to rush their throws to try to gun him down.

ICHIRO SUZUKI
RIGHT FIELDER

SEATTLE MARINERS

### STATS

Mariners seasons: 2001–present

Height: 5-foot-11

Weight: 172

- 10-time All-Star

- 10-time Gold Glove winner

- .331 career BA

- 383 career stolen bases

## MANAGER · LOU PINIELLA

Lou Piniella, nicknamed "Sweet Lou," was a fiery left fielder with a pretty swing. Piniella manned the outfield for the expansion Seattle Pilots and then played for the Orioles, Indians, Royals, and Yankees in the 1970s before launching a successful managerial career. Piniella went on to become the winningest manager in Mariners history, gaining his 234th victory on May 22, 1996, against the Boston Red Sox. Piniella was a brilliant game strategist; however, his explosive temper made him one of the most frequently ejected managers in big-league history. Piniella once threw second base into the outfield during an argument with an umpire.

**LOU PINIELLA**
MANAGER

SEATTLE
MARINERS

### STATS

**Mariners seasons as manager: 1993–2002**

**Managerial record: 1,835–1,713**

**AL West championships: 1995, 1997, 2001**

# KING FELIX REIGNS

he Mariners entered the 2005 season with Mike Hargrove as manager and a rebuilt lineup that featured longtime pitcher Jamie Moyer and a pair of sluggers in third baseman Adrian Beltre and 6-foot-6 first baseman Richie Sexson. Hargrove, who had led the Indians past the Mariners in the 1995 ALCS, believed in the team's chances for speedy improvement. "I'm encouraged by what we've got," he said, "but we have to be consistent from day one."

Hargrove and the Mariners found 2005 a tough season to endure, finishing 69–93 and at the bottom of the AL West standings. But on the bright side, the team called up from the minors 18-year-old Venezuelan pitcher Felix Hernandez, a flamethrowing right-hander with a penchant for ringing up strikeouts. Although he went just 4–4 that season, Hernandez at times demonstrated dazzling stuff, giving Mariners fans something to get excited about.

Seattle's 2006 season marked improvement, and in 2007, the Mariners assembled an 88–74 record that had them challenging for the

AL West title. A slew of new standouts had emerged, such as slugging outfielder Raúl Ibañez, stingy relief pitcher J. J. Putz, and budding catcher Kenji Johjima, the first Japanese-born backstop to sign with a major-league team. But the club's forward movement came to a halt with a severely disappointing 2008 season in which the Mariners suffered injuries and underachieving play on their way to a dreadful 61–101 record.

Following that season, the Mariners made a new start while reconnecting with their past. They hired as their new manager Don Wakamatsu, who became the first Asian-American skipper in the majors. They also brought Ken Griffey Jr. back home by signing him to a free-agent contract. "If I'm a young player on this ballclub, I've got to be pretty excited," said Seattle general manager Jack Zduriencik. "I'm going to have my ears open, I'm going to listen to what he says, and I'm going to watch him. He's going to bring a lot to the table that you're not going to be able to measure in the box score."

Sure enough, the Mariners made a 24-win improvement in 2009 as the aging but still big-swinging Junior walloped 19 homers, Ichiro kept on hitting, and "King" Felix rose to prominence with an AL-best 19–5 record. Unfortunately, Griffey retired in 2010, and the Mariners slumped.

# SPECTACULAR SAFECO

Since hosting its first Mariners game on July 15, 1999, Safeco Field has gained a reputation locally and nationally as one of baseball's most beautiful and fan-friendly stadiums. The venue offers not only sweeping, panoramic views of the Seattle skyline and summer sunsets, but excellent viewing angles of the on-field action from any seat in the house. The ballpark's one-of-a-kind retractable roof opens and closes like a well-vented convertible, covering the stands and the field but preserving an open-air environment. The structure of Safeco Field covers nearly nine acres and contains enough steel to build a skyscraper 55 stories tall, while the playing field features real Kentucky bluegrass and a specially designed watering system that resembles a spider web. Other unique features include cedar-lined dugouts, elevated bullpens, 11 video display boards, an old-fashioned, hand-operated scoreboard, and many high-tech kiosks and luxury suites equipped with Internet access. The stadium features a wide walking and viewing concourse area that allows fans to make a complete circle of the park while snacking on such fare as salmon sandwiches, clam chowder, and sushi rolls. Works of art such as a sculpture of 1,000 bats suspended above the grand staircase at the Home Plate Gate also decorate the unique ballpark.

Outfielder Milton Bradley gave the Mariners a bit of speed and power in 2010, but the club missed the playoffs for a ninth straight season.

FELIX HERNANDEZ

While Chone Figgins (below) stole 42 bases in 2010, Felix Hernandez (opposite) captured the Cy Young Award as the league's best pitcher.

Despite the speed of Ichiro and second baseman Chone Figgins, the sure fielding of center fielder Franklin Gutierrez, and the magnificent hurling of Hernandez, Seattle went just 61–101. "At the end of the day, to come up with results like this, that's very tough as a player," said Ichiro.

The Seattle Mariners have been sailing the seas of major league baseball for parts of five decades, enduring many choppy waters while getting only occasional glimpses of paradise. As today's Mariners continue trying to chart a way to their first World Series, Seattle fans patiently await the day the Emerald City's summertime heroes will sail to the ultimate baseball triumph.

CHONE FIGGINS

MARINERS